PUNCH LINES

PUNCH LINES

by

Charles Keller

illustrated by

V.G. McWilliams

Prentice-Hall, Inc., Englewood Cliffs, New Jersey

Printed in the United States of America • J

Prentice-Hall International, Inc., London
Prentice-Hall of Australia, Pty. Ltd., North Sydney
Prentice-Hall of Canada, Ltd., Toronto
Prentice-Hall of India Private Ltd., New Delhi
Prentice-Hall of Japan, Inc., Tokyo

Library of Congress Cataloging in Publication Data

Keller, Charles.
Punch lines.

SUMMARY: A number of stories told using one play on words after another.
1. [Puns and punning] I. McWilliams, V. G. II. Title.
PZ8.7.K42Pu 75-11621

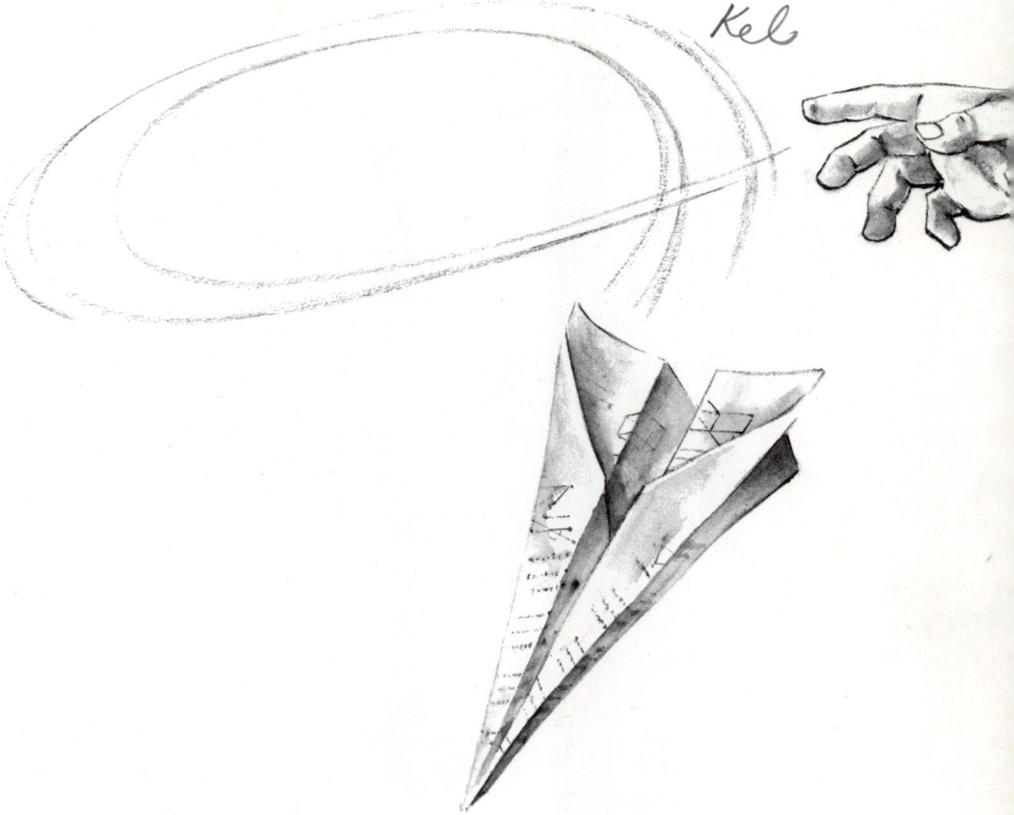

Special thanks to
Rondo, The Colonel and Eddie

PUNCH LINES

My friends and I formed a band about a week ago. I have a feeling we are going to score in the big time. That's why we want to practice every night. We play with the windows open so we get the feeling of having an audience. We are sure people on the street get a bang out of our stuff, so we pitch it as loud as we can.

I am beginning to wonder, though, if the next-door neighbor is in tune with us. Something seems wrong with hymn. Sonata big deal, but a few nights ago he tied his dog to our porch. We didn't mind the howls. Actually it was sort of like having a singer to accompany. After a while we got it alto-gether.

The next night we heard our neighbor blowing his trombone. Since we needed another brass, we called over to him to hop on our bandwagon. We think he just didn't want to horn in on us.

Two nights ago he set up his stereo on his patio. I don't know whether he was playing Braythoven or Guy Bombardo, but it was really loud. I'd be a lyre if I didn't say *we* probably sounded viol together too. But it didn't seem like anything to harp on. He was doing his thing. We were doing ours.

Last night was the finale. It *coda* been our best playing yet, except for one thing. We were blowing up a storm when, all of a sudden, there was a drumming on the door. We were too hot to stop. But with our last chord the front door fell in. It was the police. Were they ever in a zither!

They took away our instruments, saying something about having an obbligato to restore the piece. How bass do you have to be to make treble for serious musicians! I think we octave demanded an apology.

I went to the zoo yesterday. I just wanted to monkey around for a while. It was a boar. I am not lion to you.

Moose of the keepers were wolves. They would weasel at all the girls. And I saw one eager beaver ask someone to possum water for him so he could build a dam.

Another keeper went ape over a rich lady who gnu him. He tried to burro a buck from her for peanuts. "Oh deer, ocelot of money. You otter know I can't afford that much." But he

kept badgering her ferret. Finally she gave him the doe. "Be sure you pay me back," she said. "I don't want to be cheetah-d."

These are the fox: The animals were on strike. Management said the show had to go on, so the keepers were put in the cages. They seemed to bear it pretty well. Some were laughing like hyenas, although there was one with a sheepish grin—the black sheep of his family.

I had cold feet when I went to the doctor's a weak back. I was ill-advised to go there.

First thing, he said he had a bone to pick with me. "Go ahead. Your treat," I said. That made him sore, so he started giving me the needle.

"This will be a shot in the arm for you," he said.

"Cut it out," I shouted. "You make me sick and tired." Did he ever jump down my throat at that. He was a real pill. A pain in the neck, too.

Next he began to chew my ear off. I never saw anyone so vein. He said he has a real operation there. That had me in stitches. I had already boned up on him and knew there were skeletons in his closet. "You're pulling my leg," I said.

By then he was getting under my skin. "You fracture me. Now give me my bill," I said. I thought I would split a gut. He had charged an arm and a leg. "Have a heart, doc. What do you want, blood?"

I went home black and blue after rubbing elbows with him.

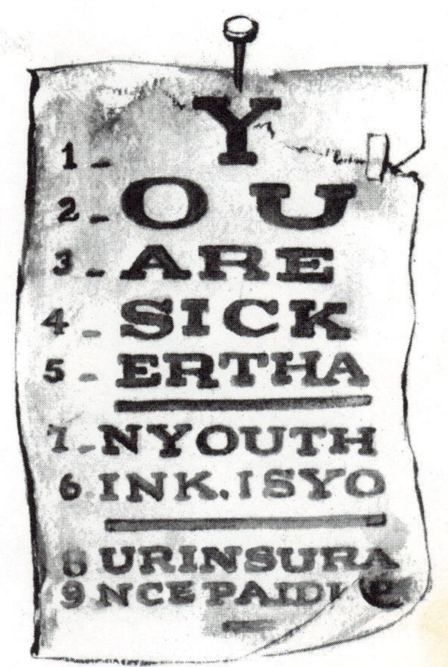

-est,

Every morning come
2 the vege- market
-coz of U.
I yam over U. Your
adorable turnip & curly
hair make U the
of my . My beets
4 U. Weed be A Great .
Do th-INK I'm a
. HON-EY -dew U Love me?
If U all 4 me, Lettuce

marrieD. Do set A date.

U glad i askeD?

Don't S-A we  -taloupe. I earn only a small  but i wood Give U  and quiet.

Don't say U artichoke Me. That wood 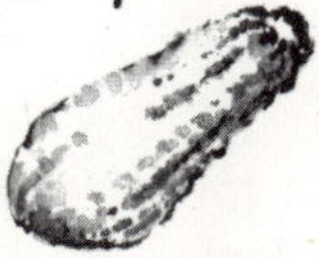 ME. Nothing will Ev.R spiNAch my LOVE 4 you. Please Don't Give ME the  . I'll alwaze  U.

Kumquat may, i  you.

URZ in melon-choly,

I had a little bit of trouble at the soupermarket the other day. Aisle tell you about it.

I had a coupon worth 10¢ on a package of heat-and-eat hotcakes. Just as I reached for the last box on the shelf, wham, some big oaf grabbed it. Usually it takes a lot to jar me. I keep my feelings bottled up. But this took the cake. "You sugar got your nerve," Ice creamed. "That's my box."

"Put a lid on it, kid," he said. "I don't want any sauce from you."

I don't relish a fight. But this time I mustard all my strength and took a good pork at him. He landed hard in the soft drinks. You never sausage a mess.

The manager came running over. He really had the goods on us. I figured he was going to give us the sack. For once I used my noodle. I knew I was in a jam so I decided to butter him up. "Check out the facts. I creamed the big cheese because he grabbed my hotcakes. No juice crying over spilled milk, is there?"

"I'll count up to ten," the manager said, "and if you two aren't out of here by then, I'll call the police. And don't ever cumin here egg-ain."

BIG
SALE
-NOW-
HEAT 'N' EAT 'EM

Auntie's Volkswagen broke down a few days ago. I told her she auto turn it in to the old volks' home, but that choked her up. She said she wasn't ready to re-tire it, that it still had a lot of good miles on it. So we had it towed to the gas station.

I knew she would be taken for a ride there. Right off, the mechanic said he didn't want to o-fender, but her car needed a lot of work done on it. I tried to pump him for details, but he pretended not to know what I was driving at. Axle-ly he was just stalling while he figured how much he could

jack up the charges. I wanted to throttle him, but he made auntie a flat promise, "Wheel do the best job in town. We don't skid around. We'll grease your car from headlights to tailpipe. And we won't brake your budget. We use only second-hand parts. After oil, it's fuelish not to economize these days."

Auntie tanked him and said she would return the next day to pick the car up.

I got the shock of my life when we went back. The car looked like a rolling junk heap. But auntie is really plugged into it. "This gas to be the only one of its kind," she said. She now spins a propellor to start it and throws out an anchor to stop it, but she says it runs like a sewing machine—with a treadle.

See all the stories it has
LIBRARY
1. I went to the library.
A sight for sore eyes
Bess Seller
LIBRARIAN
2. I saw the librarian.
3. She was all write with me. That was one book I was going to judge by its cover.
READ ANY GOOD BOOKS LATELY?
X
(MY IMPRINT)
4. I wanted an introduction, so I tried a novel approach.
5. To make a long story short, I had a tiger by the tale.
Will Mr. Imprint please report to the front desk
AT ONCE!
6. She had me paged.

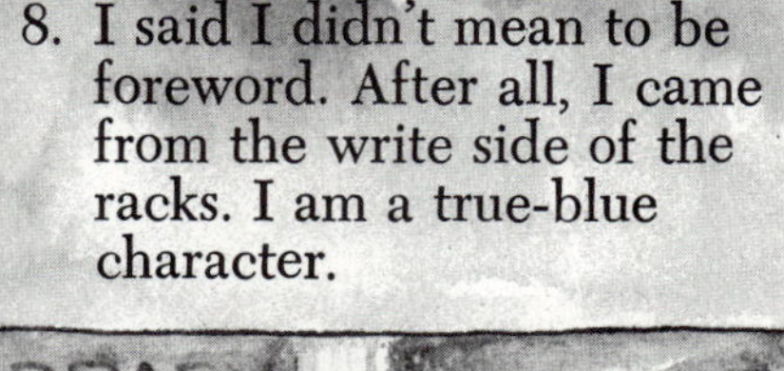

8. I said I didn't mean to be foreword. After all, I came from the write side of the racks. I am a true-blue character.

10. She said she was booked solid. And that was the end.

11. I'm turning over a new leaf. Nothing binding, you understand. Now my motto is: Know Thy Shelf.

12. Tonight I am going to improve my mind.

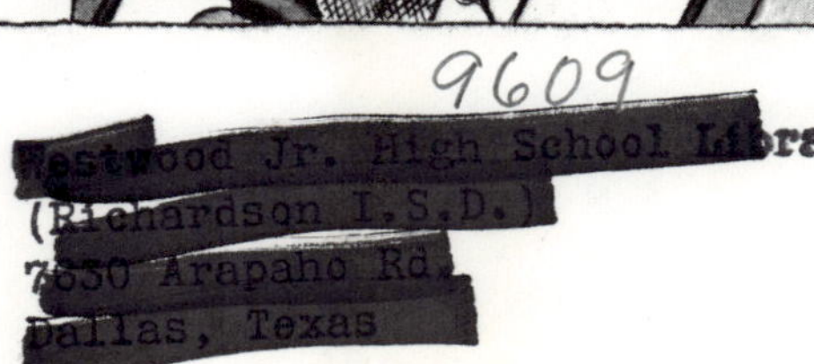

I was on my way to a pressing engagement on the outskirts of town when I noticed a spot on my sleeve. I stopped at a neighborhood tailor shop and buttonholed the owner. I put him on the spot. "Can you take it out?" I asked.

"Not if it's on the cuff," he replied.

I thought he was trying to needle me, so I started to give him a dressing down. He said to keep my shirt on, that he just wanted to be sure I had nothing up my sleeve. In his business he has to play it clothes to the vest.

With that, he poured remover on the spot. Press-to, the spot turned orange. "You're doing just sew-sew," I told him. I was on pins and needles to get to my appointment on time.

"Let's give it another coat," he said. When the steam cleared, the spot was gone. And so was the sleeve.

I was fit to be tied. "I ought to cuff you," I said as I collared him. "How can I face an interview with just one sleeve?"

"Don't be depressed. We'll iron this out for you. Every cloud has a silver lining."

"I don't want a silver lining. I want a sleeve. Mend it. How you do it is immaterial. But it had better suit me."

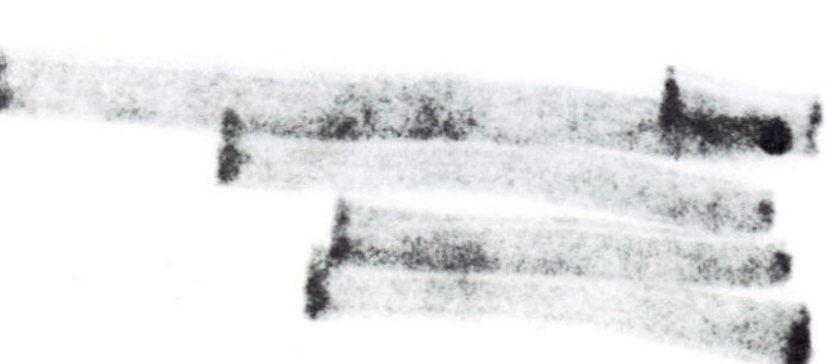

WELCOME

Wood you believe it, yesterday I watched a house being built. The fellow who was putting it up had really climbed the ladder. I figured that talking to him would cement our relationship. Not that there was anything concrete between us. It is just that I saw opportunity knocking when he put out the welcome mat.

Dig this. When he first started out, his back was against the wall. His business was on the rocks. He was in the hole. Everyone was trying to ditch him. Troubles piled on him like a ton of bricks. He was floored. Then when he found that other builders were trying to frame him, he hit the ceiling. But then he hit pay dirt. Now he is scooping it in. That's how you window.

This man is on the level. He is not plastered. His advice hits the nail on the head. He says there is always room at the top. "Attic your problems. Raise the roof."

So that is where I am putting my foundations. I'm building blocks every day from now on.

THE Toy

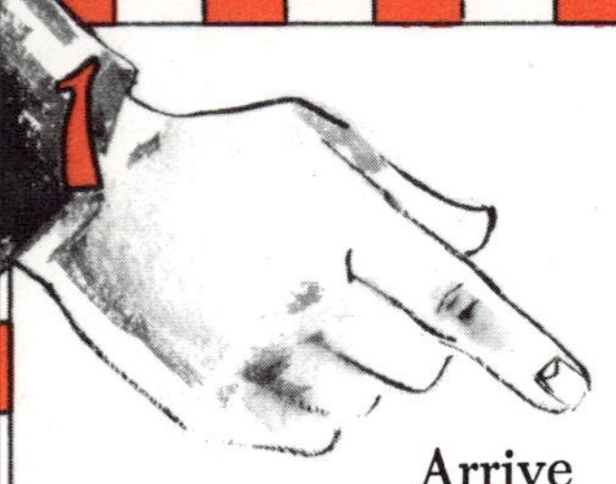

1

Arrive at toy store. Do not play around.

Advance to #2

2

Tell owner you wish to talk to his daughter.

Proceed to #4
Do not stop on way.

3

The owner's daughter is a gifted kid and a real doll.

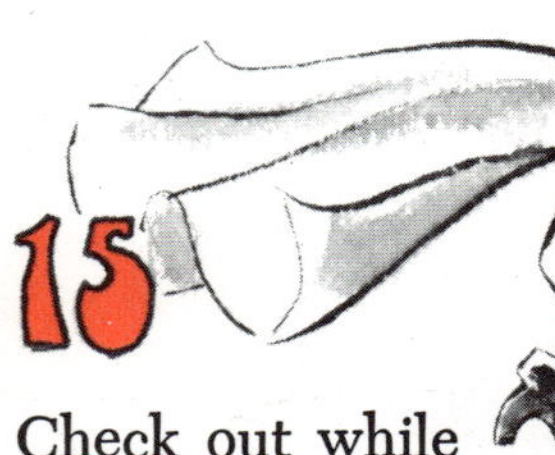

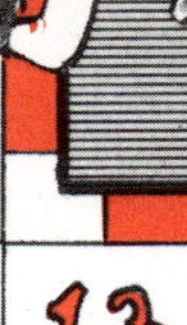

15

Check out while you are still a jump ahead of him.

14

Owner says he must get something off his chess.

Say "No dice. I'm board."

See him pail at #15 . . .

13

"Model yourself after me. Be a big shot."

If you get a bang out of that, spend the night in jail. Otherwise go to #14.

12

Why not string him along instead.

And hear him say at #13 . . .

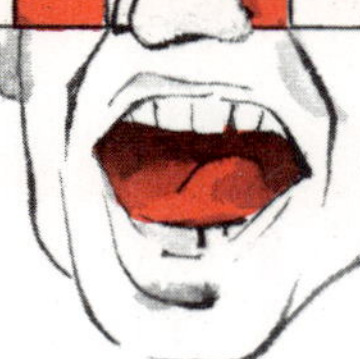

You receive a balling out from the owner.

Go to #5 to see why.

He says, "A good skate you aren't."

If you see his game, move on to #6.

He aims to put you behind the 8 ball with her.

Collect your wits and shout . . .

7

"Nobody toys with me. I'm leaving."

Open door to dart out.

Hear owner say, "Don't go. I've got a deal for you."

Hear more on #10

10

"I have a monopoly on this business. You should train for it."

Control yourself. Say, "And have you taken me for a ride?"

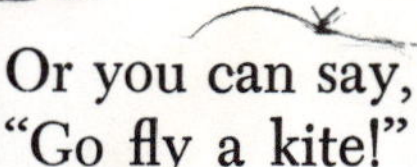

Or you can say, "Go fly a kite!"

I went to the lake to rent a boat last Sunday. The fellow who ran the boathouse was a real drink of water. Perhaps he had been trying to drown his sorrows because he wasn't navigating too well. Or maybe he just hadn't gotten his sea legs for the day.

"Canoe rent me a skiff?" I asked. No answer. "What's up, dock? Did you miss the boat?" He didn't get the drift of it. He was a stick in the mud, for shore. I could sea I would have to make waves to get a boat. This time I was stern. "What's the hitch? I want a boat, the schooner the better."

"Shove off, sailor," he said and port himself a drink. I didn't aft to be dry behind the ears to see he was all wet.

"I didn't come here to get in to a row," I said. "But I am going to have a boat oar I am going to know why." I was trying to keep my anchor to myself. It was knot easy. I knew, though, that I would be in over my head if I went off the deep end.

"I am taking the one tide up here," I said. And I jumped in. I made a splash all right. I went through the bottom. It was not a boat worth wading for.

I think the owner of the hardware store has a few screws loose. He is always in the back of the store dozing when customers come in. Something must be nailing him. On the level, though, this is what I saw there the other day.

I was pretty burned up when he didn't come out to wait on me. Some of my sparks ignited a rope attached to the ceiling. The resulting flame (A) burned through the rope causing (B) a cement block tied to the rope to (C) drop on the bellows directly underneath. The sudden burst of air (D) from the bellows fanned the fire (E) in nearby boiler, building up pressure (F) and causing compressor (G) to start ceiling fan (H). Fan made sticky flypaper (I) flap wildly. Flypaper brushed against

owner's hairpiece and (J) yanked it from his head. Cold air blowing on his head woke up owner, who then sat bolt upright and clamped his wig back on.

"Wire you looking at me that way?" he asked.

"The plane truth," I said, "is that I thought you wood think you had been chiseled out of your nap and you'd blow a fuse."

That gave him a charge. He laughed and said he was awl ready to get down to brass tacks.

"Brace yourself," I said. "It's a light bulb I want." Then I went out, solder but wiser.

I always have trouble when I take tests. Yesterday I had finals in arithmetic and geography. You can probably guess what happened.

I have a math teacher who is a Spain in the neck. I Troy to be Seville to her, but it dozen seem to make any difference. One of her questions went like this: If Mrs. Black has ten ears of corn and each ear takes ten minutes to cook, when will the Blacks have supper.

I got 'X' for saying the corn wouldn't cook until the water was Berlin. Norway for it to be done faster.

Then there was another one about somebody named Bob who was making three bookshelves, and how much lumber would he need for five shelves.

I said every little bit Alps.

Yukon see I was confused. The teacher called me to her desk after class and said, "Alaska question. What has gotten India. Can't Jamaica your mind what class you are in?" There was Somoa but I won't Goa into it. Finally she said she was Finnish. So Iran out.

When I got to my geography class the teacher was counting to ten. She had my paper in front of her. I knew my number was up. "What is your angle," she said. "This is a geography test, but you make it sound like a math paper. The Red Sea is not famous for dividing. And whoever heard of Asia Minus? It's Asia Minor. Mark my words, if this is how you solve your problems, you will never make the grade in my class. I am positive you have a negative attitude. To sum it up, I can't give you even a fraction of a zero for this paper."

And to sum her up, her Maine talent is keeping me in Missouri.

HAW
HO
HEH-HEH
HA-A-A.
TROPHY
I don't give a HOOOoo-t
You're

PEOPLE
PEOPLE!
OWARDLY CHICKEN
IT'S ALL
A LOT OF
MANWASH
Cat
who let
gossip out
of the bag
SOUTHERN
FRIED
COLONEL
SARDINES
STEAM-PACKED
COMMUTER-STYLE

We were in the mood for a whale of a time last night, so my friends and I went to the seafood place down by the river. Holy mackerel, was it crowded! People were packed in like sardines. It was hot and noisy. The band played only one song, "Salmon Enchanted Evening." Is it from *Porgy and Bass?* Anyhow, the singers called themselves the Tuna Fishes. They were so flat it would have been nice to have been hard of herring. What's more, the place had a fishy smelt. I was beginning to feel green around the gills. It was sel-fish of me, but I wished we hadn't come.

Finally we were taken to a table. The minnow was brought, and we floundered around trying to decide what to order. I asked the waiter if they had sole food. What a crab he was. Perhaps he was eel, or maybe he had a haddock. He looked me up and down and said, "Small fry, it costs a fin, and you just don't look to me like you live on that scale." I was sharked. I would like to have gotten my hooks into him, but since he had big mussels, I clammed up. Our porpoise in going there was to have a good time, not to get in to hot water. It made no sense to carp. I decided to perch up and have a good time.

With a flourish I told the waiter I wanted blue fish. I should have known better. I finally had to take the fish home to cheer him up. And that made me shad.

Yesterday I went to the dentist. I had heard about him by word of mouth. Somebody said he was of English extraction, but I am sure he's an American, a Yank—with a lot of pull, too.

My appointment was at tooth-hurty. When I walked in he said, "Long time no fee. Abcess makes the heart grow fonder." I told him to hold his tongue and get to the root of my problem.

He began to drill. I think he was bored to tears. I asked him if he was biting off more than he could chew. "What a gas," he said.

"Right," said I. "Fill 'er up." That had him in stitches. He claims he is very painstaking in his work. He feels his duty is to the whole tooth and nothing but the tooth.

I don't believe him. His other patients don't believe him ether.

1. The announcer who does the weather forecasts on television is a big bag of wind.

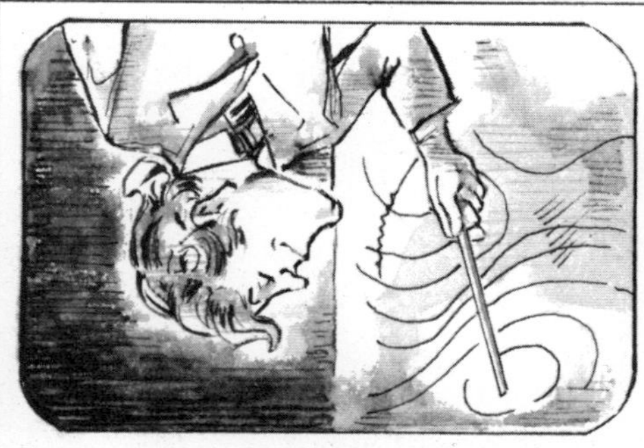

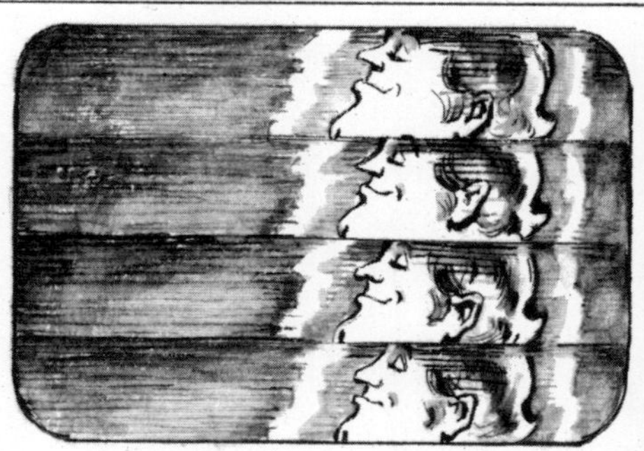

2. He's balmy. Watch him put on airs. It's all a front, though.

3. He pretends he has a sunny disposition. But I happen to know he is always in a fog.

4. He doesn't have enough sense to come in out of the rain.

5. I'd like to know where he hails from because he is always under the weather.

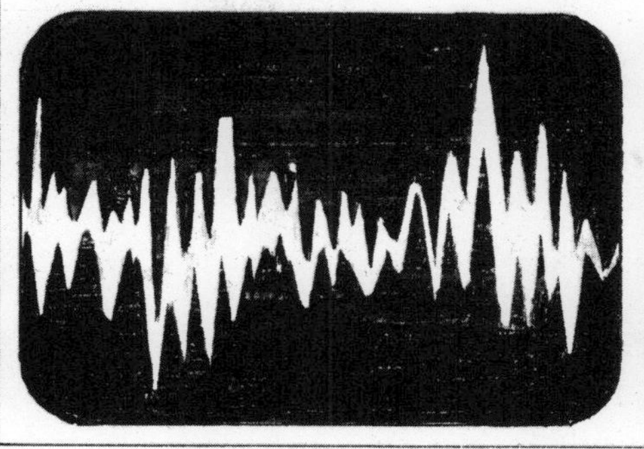

See your local newspaper for today's forecast.

6. Somebody ought to pressure him to clear out. But I drought he will fall for that. He is very unseasonable.

Things would be different if I had his job. I wouldn't just shoot the breeze, and I wouldn't do a snow job. You would get a fair forecast from me, weather you liked it or not.

If anyone stormed in to complain I'd tell them, "You can always beat the heat if you don't blow your cool."

SONNY
the weather fore-
caster's daughter
MARK
the teacher's son
SHERRY
the wine seller's
daughter
PHIL
the dentist's son
RED
the librarian's son
SUE and WILL
the lawyer's twins
HONEY
the beekeeper's
daughter
BILL
.15
.40
.75
$5.20
KITTY
the pet-shop
owner's daughter
BILL
the waiter's son
GRACE
the minister's daughter
CRYSTAL
the watch-
maker's daughter
ART
the painter's son
EMIL
the restaurant
owner's son

12 x 10 = 120
13 x 10 = 130
= 136
OSCAR
the actor's son
PATIENCE
the doctor's daughter
JACK
the automobile
mechanic's son
RICH
the millionaire's son
VIOLET, ROSE,
LILY and DAISY
the florist's daughters
CLAY
the sculptor's son
JIM
the basketball player's
son
STU
the cook's son
MIKE
the announcer's son
SPIKE
the railroad man's son
ANNETTE and ROD
the fisherman's children
Class members missing
the day photographs
were taken:
ROB, the thief's son,
who was on a job;
CLIFF, the mountain
climber's son, home
with a broken leg;
WOODY and CHIP, the
carpenter's boys;
EARL, the gas station
owner's son;
MOE, whose father cuts
the grass at the coun-
try club.

I take my hat off to my barber. He knows how to get ahead in his business even if he never seems to know who is necks.

He always teases me, calls me little shaver. It gives him a bang when I yell, "Aw, comb on now."

He lets his hair down with customers. They tell him to cut it short, but he pretends not to hear. He always tells the same old stories. There is one about a fellow who asked for a close shave but who was afraid to take it on the chin. And there is another about a customer who tried to razor stink because he had a nick on his mug. He was in a lather because he thought the barber had the edge on him.

He gives the same advice to everyone.

IF YOU FALL HAIR TO A FORTUNE, YOU MOUSTACHE SOME OF IT AWAY.

IF YOU GIVE A COMB TO A BALD MAN, HE WILL NEVER PART WITH IT.

HAIR TODAY, GONE TOMORROW.

Some of his customers say he gets in their hair. They blow their tops when that happens. They say he gives them a scalping without really cutting their hair.

The barber just smiles and brushes them off.

I took my date to the ball game last night. The ball park is just a shortstop from the station. It's a cool place to go because they have fans in every seat.

I had decided the time had come to make a grandstand play for her. She's a good sport and we usually hit it off pretty well, but I have never been able to get to first base with her.

Right off the bat I started making my pitch. Maybe it was a little hit or miss, but there were no catches to it. I'm not the kind to throw curves to anyone. At first she let it slide even though she had to run. I told her she was a diamond in the rough. I wanted her to know she was driving me bats.

Well, that was the big-inning of the end. She told me that I wasn't in her league . . . that I batter take a walk if I didn't want to be knocked out of the box. She said she knew the score . . . that I was in error . . . way off base . . . also out in left field. She didn't say I was a foul ball, but she might as well have.

In short, I struck out.

The only thing for me to do was run home.

Now I'll never catcher.